THIS IS A WORK OF NON-FICTION. SOME NAMES AND IDENTIFYING DETAILS HAVE BEEN CHANGED TO PROTECT THE PRIVACY OF INDIVIDUALS.

How I Survived Working at RTD/Metro (Watch Your Back!)

Darlene Thompson

Afflatus Press Publishing

Thousand Oaks, CA 91362

How I Survived Working at RTD/Metro

By Darlene Thompson

Copyright @ 2019 Darlene Thompson

ALL RIGHTS RESERVED

First Printing – December 2019

ISBN:

NO PART OF THIS BOOK MAY BE REPRODUCED IN ANY FORM, BY PHOTOCOPYING OR BY ANY ELECTRONIC OR MECHANICAL MEANS, INCLUDING INFORMATION STORAGE OR RETRIEVAL SYSTEMS, WITHOUT PERMISSION IN WRITING FROM THE COPYRIGHT OWNER/AUTHOR.

Printed In the USA

ACKNOWLEDGEMENTS

To my Amazing Son De'Onzae Thompson, who I love unconditionally, every battle I won was a battle won for us. To my Mother and Father, thank you for encouraging me to follow my dream and write this book about my life at RTD/METRO. To Kristen Gray, one of my dearest friends, who planted the seed fourteen years ago that I should write a book about my life on the job. Special Thanks to my publisher and sister Asia Jackson. I couldn't have done this without you. To my family and friends, thank you for your support and encouraging words. I love you to the moon and back.

TABLE OF CONTENTS

Intro	8
Eager	13
Nineteen	16
Perm on Premises	19
A Man in Uniform	22
No Loyalty	28
I Spy	33
Slip'n On the Job	35
Fake Cake and Ice Cream	37
New Booties	40
Snap-Crackle-Pop	42
The Stank is Real	49
Finally Enough	52
All Food Ain't Good Food	56
Some-Timey Co-workers	58
Rainy Night	60
Shop Steward	62
Exposed	65
Sister in Christ	68

Town Crier	72
Fifty Hands	74
My Wife is Black	77
A Fool	82
Princess of Metro	90
Diamonds Who Care	95
No One But God	99

Intro

I remember it as if it was yesterday. It was August 31, 1987, I was 19 years old, excited about working for RTD as a service attendant and above minimum wage. My starting pay was $10.85 an hour. I thought, with this job, I can begin to help my mom, take her on vacation to the Bahamas and buy myself a 325 BMW.

I was a little nervous working in the real world straight out of high school. I had always worked with peers my own age. It was a new experience to work around grown-ups. I thought this would be great. I made sure to show them respect by not addressing them as I would teenagers. I felt blessed to be starting my career so young, so I made up my mind to pass the probation period even if I had to catch the bus every day to work and be there two hours before my shift. Being late was not an option.

My first day of work, everyone was so nice and full of welcoming and friendly smiles. Everyone was giving advice and telling me what it would take to pass probation. They also told me that once I passed probation I would be in the union, have medical benefits, and a supervisor or manager could not fire or suspend me without a very good reason. I was the youngest among my co-workers and they gave me the nicknames "Microwave Baby" and "She's a Baby," which I didn't like.

They called me "Microwave Baby" because, well, at 19, I didn't know how to cook. So when all the workers brought food for an event like a holiday or a birthday party, I would bring something I bought at the store. I didn't know how to cook anything. I hated being called "Microwave Baby."

A pest named Jerome was my co-worker and he often acted like he was the boss of me. He would tell me what to do and how to do it every day. This man got on my nerves but I wasn't sure if I could tell him to go kick rocks.

Then one day, I had enough of him harassing me about not washing down the fuel island properly, so I went to my lead person Jackie and told her how he was bothering me and telling me how I'm not doing my job correctly. She said, "What? He's not your leader. Come with me, Darnene." Well, my name is Darlene, but I didn't say anything. Jackie was the first person I ever knew who couldn't pronounce my name. I thought my name was easy to pronounce.

Anyway, I followed her and as she approached Jerome. She told him: "You talk too much, you need to shut up and mind your own business." When I saw how he just stood there with his mouth closed and how she had punked him, that was the last day his scary self would ever try to bully me. He tried of course but I put him in his place and reminded him that he is not my leader. A few years later he resigned from RTD and took the test to become a firefighter.

There was a lady service attendant named Maya. She was a very pretty lady. I would speak to her but she would ignore me every day. She reminded me of high school girls when they don't like someone.

This guy named Griffin loved to play around with Maya, then one day his focus switched to me. Griffin would always try to trap me in the bale-room, he would stand in front of me blocking my path. I would tell him to move, to let me by, but he kept playing with me and not letting me walk by. He had me blocked between the stairs and the door of the bale-room and I couldn't move. I felt like crying but I didn't. I could see Maya in the background, looking pleased that I was frustrated. That was the first time I ever saw a smile on her face. That's when I knew, this lady doesn't like me. I stayed away from her as much as possible.

Growing up, my mom always taught my siblings and me to respect our elders. The grown-ups I was around didn't act foolish or carry themselves in an unbecoming manner. To my surprise, this was not the case with a lot of RTD employees. The bus drivers were loud, walking around like high school kids. I could hear them coming down the hallway speaking loudly, saying things like: "Hey, baby, what's going on?" They were louder than my high school friends sitting on the quad. That was the beginning of me realizing that age isn't nothing but a number; you have old and young fools.

One day this lady bus driver came into the locker room where I was taking my break. She and I had never had a conversation before, we just would say hi and bye to each other. She asked me: "Why when you're asleep in bed, men like to stick it from behind?" I couldn't answer that question. I was nineteen years old, still living at home. I just sat there trying to look normal but, on the inside, I was screaming with my hands over my ears, thinking, "Lady, I don't want to hear this!" I realized people don't care if you're nineteen years old. You work in a grown-up environment and you expect people are going to talk and approach you as an adult. I know, I know, I was so green when I started with the company.

Eager

You would think people that are already established in life would be happy to see the younger generation come in and make a better life for themselves. Nope, not at all. The people I worked with at RTD, from the managers, supervisors, mechanics, to the service attendants were waiting for your demise. When you first start working for RTD, you are on probation for four months. That means you can be fired if you are absent or late or if the lead person speaks bad about your work performance. Break any of these rules and you are terminated.

Let me give you the back story. When I was 18 years old I entered the Kenneth Hahn youth graffiti program. The program paid minimum wage, which was $4.25 an hour. The service attendant would drive us around to different bus layovers. It was about five of us to a van, we would get out and get our bottle of graffiti spray and paper towels and clean off the graffiti inside of the buses. I did that job for one year and received an employee badge number.

After a year of cleaning graffiti, RTD gave us a chance to take the test for service attendant. In order to become a service attendant, I had to take off work from the graffiti job and I got the OK from my boss because she knew it was work-related. I took three days, one to take the test, another to get a printout of my driving record and another to interview for the position.

After I became a service attendant, three months into it, I overheard a supervisor say to another supervisor: "We got her." As I walked in the office he gave me a hearing letter and said I had to meet with him and the manager. I didn't know what was going on; I knew I hadn't done anything but I was still nervous. I did not want a hearing while on probation.

The day of the hearing, they showed me a printout of all the days I worked for RTD. My time with the graffiti program was also included. There seems to have been some confusion because my badge number in my new position was the same number I had in the graffiti program. They thought they had me because of the days I had skipped when I was still in the graffiti program even though all of the graffiti program dates were in the month of June and my starting date with RTD was August 31, 1987.

You should have seen the supervisor's face after I

explained everything. He looked so confused and out done. He looked so stupid; if he hadn't been so eager to get me terminated and looked at the printout closely, he would have realized I didn't even work for the company on those dates. SMH. Once the meeting was over, I kept a straight face, thinking to myself, "Fool, you don't have me, but I got you."

Nineteen

There was a pretty Latino lady bus driver named Patty. All the guys were crazy about her. As she would walk across the yard to her assigned bus, the men service attendants and mechanics would always stare at her. I thought it was funny how one minute they would be talking to each other and when Patty walked by, they would stop talking or stop whatever they were doing just to look at her. She seemed to be a friendly person, she would always say hi or good morning to me in passing and I would reply back.

One day I went to the candy machine inside the Transportation Department and as I was walking through the door, I saw Patty and she looked at me and winked at me. In those seconds I didn't know what to do or how to respond. I hurried and looked away and turned my body facing the candy machine. I was nineteen at the time and never encountered that from a girl or woman. From that day I felt nervous to be around her because she would look at me the way a guy would when he was being flirtatious. I didn't know how to handle this type of situation, so whenever I would see her, I just acted like I didn't know she was flirting with me.

One day I got sick on the job. At that time I was catching the bus to work, so my supervisor called transportation to see if they had any bus drivers that could take me home in a car-unit. He told me they had a driver and to go to the Transportation Department to meet her. Guess who it was taking me home? Yep, you guessed right, it was Patty. I wanted to say "Nooooo, not her" but I didn't. I put on a brave face and got into the car-unit. She asked me for directions to my house. We had general conversation. I remember her telling me she went to an all-girl school and I was thinking: "Is that where it first happened, you liking girls?"

As we approached my home, I told her to slow down, this is my home right here. She put the car in park with the motor still running and I thanked her for giving me a ride home. Patty was doing good not flirting with me the whole time until I opened the car door and she put her hand on my thigh. I felt so uncomfortable. I played it off as if she didn't just cross the line. I told her how to take the freeway back to the job and got out of the car as quickly as I could.

At some point she transferred to another work location and I didn't see her again for years. When Patty transferred back to my work location,

I was thirty-something, married and had a child. Patty's looks had changed; she didn't look feminine anymore. She carried herself more like a dude, her hairstyle was even different. Her haircut reminded me of Erik Estrada from the TV show ChiPs. Patty did not flirt with me right away but one day as I was leaving the locker room, she was coming in, so I stepped aside so she could pass. Instead of passing by, she stepped to the side, looking me in my eyes, and I stepped to the opposite side, so she stepped in front of me again. Now I'm pissed. I said, "What do you think you're doing? Don't play with me. I don't play that shit." Her expression changed to anger and she got out of my way and I left. From that day forward I never had any problems with Patty again.

PERM ON THE PREMISES

After I passed probation, I was on the day shift four months before getting bumped to graveyard shift. I had already heard from the day shift that graveyard supervisor Greg was loud and crazy. Little did I know Greg was one of the nicest supervisors I had ever met. Greg walked with a limp. It is true Greg would walk up and down the mechanic shop hollering and fussing about nothing. I believe Greg wanted people to think he was crazy.

I had to catch the bus every day to work and I would get to work sometimes two hours before starting time. I would go in the lunch room to watch TV until it was time to punch in. One night I was sitting in the lunch room when Greg saw me from down the hallway, and he shouted out, "Baby, where do you live, you're in here too early every day, we have to find someone who lives in your area that can give you a ride to work and back home." I told him where I lived and he found someone that lived five minutes from my home. He was an older man, and also a service attendant. His name was Tony. He was a nice man. I became really good friends with him and his wife.

Supervisor Greg looked out for me so much. Sometimes my co-workers would be working servicing buses at the fuel island and I would tell Greg that I had to go back to work and help them or they will be mad at me. Then he would turn on the crazy again and say, "I'm the supervisor, you don't have to go nowhere." The next thing I knew, Greg pulled out a container filled with perm relaxer, he had a black comb in his hand and he threw a towel across his shoulders. He started putting perm on his hair, then he asked me to comb it through. Now just picture me combing perm relaxer through my supervisor's hair in the manager's office. Ha!

For Greg, I did it because he was a cool guy and I had a lot of respect for him. He never tried to flirt with me. One night he asked me and this lady mechanic if we would like a fish dinner, and we both said yes.

He called up his girlfriend Tina. She was a service attendant at another location. I never met her before that night, I had just heard about her from other co-workers. Anyhow, Greg told her to bring three fish dinners. I believe she thought the other two dinners were for men mechanics because when she arrived, she got out of the car with fish dinners in hand and when Greg walked up to her, she looked hotter than fish grease. To her surprise the dinners were for a teenybopper and a blonde, white, woman mechanic. I could hear her telling Greg: "You had me come all the way down here to bring them food!" I just walked off because if looks could kill, I wouldn't be here telling you my story today. Who knew five years later Tina would transfer to my work location (oh boy), Greg had long gone and retired and moved out of state. Greg was conveniently crazy but he was a cool dude.

A Man in Uniform

From management to Transportation and the Maintenance Department, most of the men were womanizers. Bus drivers take turns dating each other, with each man having two and three girlfriends on the job and off. In management and maintenance, their girlfriends are mostly married women. Supervisors that are married date bus drivers. Married mechanics and service attendants date women on a different shift than them. This goes on at every division – just one big mess.

The women aren't any better. A lady named Victoria who was a service attendant fell on hard times and was homeless. Her friend Cindy that was a bus driver, was kind enough to let Victoria live with her until she found somewhere else to live. Victoria soon found out Cindy was dating a supervisor in the Transportation Department. While living with Cindy, Victoria started dating Cindy's boyfriend behind her back and eventually the guy left her for Victoria. Once that news spread around the division, Victoria was talked about like a dog. She had an invisible scarlet "A" on her forehead.

This type of behavior went on all of the time. She should have taken heed to the saying "Don't break the woman code." Unfortunately, when a bus driver puts on his uniform it doesn't matter if he's short, fat or unattractive, the uniform blinds these women and they can have just as many girlfriends as the decent-looking guys because all these women see is a man in uniform. Future Metro Employees Warning Alert! Don't date someone who is married or dating someone on the job because all of your business will be out there for all to know before you go back to work Monday morning! To all men in uniform: Just because a woman has a fifteen-minute conversation with you doesn't give you the green light to hug her or call her "Baby" the next time you see her.

I was working when a bus driver came up to me and started a conversation. He seemed like a nice guy, it was just a pleasant conversation, then he left. The next day I had to go to the Transportation Department to pick up car-unit keys so that I could service the cars. As I walked inside of the Transportation Department, I saw a room full of bus drivers waiting for their assigned buses and I also saw the bus driver who I talked to the day before walking towards me. As he was approaching me, he opened his arms up wide with an expression on his face that read: Give Big Daddy a hug. I looked at him with his arms wide opened and the expression on my face read: "You don't know me and why are you trying to show off in front of all of these drivers as if we have been friends for years?"

My mother had a saying for me and my siblings: "Wherever you act up, that's where you're going to get it." So, I applied that same sentiment for Metro folks. And since this man wanted to show off, he got it right there in front of his co-workers. I bypassed his wide-open arms and said, "Good morning. It doesn't take all of that," and I kept walking. That man never spoke to me again. Of course, I'm the bad person because I didn't let him play Big Daddy and put his arms around me, but I can live with that.

I wasn't always outspoken when I started working for Metro. I had to learn really fast to stand up for myself or be ate up alive by Metro employees. Some of the men and women would do things I didn't like. For instance, I was at the food truck and this bus driver came and stood next to me and uttered something, then put his arm around my shoulders. I quickly shrugged my shoulders and said, "Don't touch me!" He looked at me angrily and said, "Fuck you with your flat ass!"

Now that's something I never had - a flat ass, but I was so uncomfortable and shocked that he said that to me, I just ignored him. It really bothered me later that evening at home. I was thinking I should have told him off. He was out of line using that language and tone with me, but I did report him to my supervisor the following day. I always regretted not speaking up for myself in that moment, but I didn't like making a scene nor arguing on the job. Eventually, I got sick and tired of not speaking my mind. I got to the point where I did not care where I was or who was there; if someone disrespected me, I would let them have it and when I left the situation, I felt good because I didn't leave with the person being unchecked.

Once I started checking people on the spot, the news spread quickly. People would say I'm mean, I'm a bitch and they would tell people who I didn't have a problem with to leave me alone and don't talk to me. I don't go off on people unless they disrespect me, and people didn't tell the truth about why I had to put them in their place. They loved for people to think I just went around checking people for no reason. Sadly, I had co-workers that were followers and didn't think for themselves and believed the hype. There were a handful of co-workers that had gotten to know me for themselves, and we got along just fine. I respected them and they respected me. I no longer cared what the clique or haters thought or said about me.

I learned that being a woman on the job, it was best not to let a lot of men hug you, massage your shoulders, or place their hand on your back because other men would see it as an opportunity to follow suit and they too would try to hug and touch you and see how much they could get away with. I worked with a majority of men; can you imagine fifty men putting their arms around me every day to say good morning? That's too many damn hands for me. If you're not a friend I have known for years, you can't give me a hug. The mistake some Metro men made was thinking all women were the same. Now you did have some Metro women that loved getting hugs and attention and didn't mind you putting your hand on their shoulders or back, and that was okay if they didn't have a problem with it. When I started out with the company, I was a sunflower but after years dealing with Metro folks, I became a cactus. Ha! My motto was: "You don't have to like me, but damn it, you will respect me!"

No Loyalty

From the time I began working for Metro, I experienced no loyalty among some women. Beware, because they smile in your face and hate your guts. I found out through the years that just because a person greets you with a good morning or asks how you're doing or wishes you a good weekend, it doesn't mean they mean you any good. It's just words to say. Soon as you walk away, there's a knife in your back. They talk about you negatively, lie on you, mix the truth with lies, make shit up about you, go on a campaign to slander you and/or tell the supervisor lies about you so he can focus on you and take his attention off them.

I have met some kind, sweet-spirited women whose loyalty cannot be shaken, my friends to the end. But I have met far more two-faced women that never had good intentions.

Through the years I became a loner on the job. I didn't want to deal with negative women who pretended to be cool with me. Some women come into your life to see what's going on in your household. They're curious about you, want to know where you live, what you're doing and who you are doing on your days off so they can carry the news back to the job.

There was a clique of women who would send out a likeable person from the clique to try and talk to me, to see if I would open up. Every time this person saw me, she would ask small questions. I was always very vague in my responses. The person didn't realize I peeped out their game and the game is old, just different players. A co-worker once told me that one of the ladies asked him why he talks to me, and he responded, "Because she's nice and hasn't done anything to me." He also told me they watched everything I did, what I ate and how I walked. I know it sounds crazy, but you must be a metro employee to understand.

Let's not leave out the men. We had grown men telling other grown men not to talk to me. Isn't that weird? Men with families acting worse than women on the job. (SMH) The men were so messy and such gossipers.

I believe what rubs people the wrong way about me is that I'm not a follower and I demand respect and they can't make me feel like an outsider. I'm a loner with no interest being around messy people and I don't care if they never speak to me. I like cool, down-to-earth people, it doesn't matter if you're a manager, supervisor, lead person, service attendant, mechanic, bus driver, etc. I just like who I like, I can feel their energy and if it feels authentic and we show each other respect, that's all I care about.

My co-workers could act very strange, sometimes they would speak and sometimes they wouldn't. Some of the men liked to ensnare you into speaking to them and the next day, walk by you with their head turned in the opposite direction so they didn't have to acknowledge you. If a person did me like that more than once, I would cut that person off and not speak to him or her again. It's like a game to some people and I don't want to play. If for some reason a person doesn't want to acknowledge me, then don't! Because being some-timey doesn't work for me.

A co-worker would walk by me and not speak, and I wouldn't say anything to him either. This went on for months. One day out of the blue he decided to say hi as he walked past me. I replied hi and said, "Oh you're speaking today." He looked shocked that I called him out on his shit. He made up some story as to why he wasn't speaking. I told him it throws me off. "I never know when to say hi to you. If I feel you don't want to be bothered, I will leave you alone. So, are we speaking now?" He said yes then changed his mind and had the audacity to tell me: "Well, sometimes I won't speak."

I looked at him very calmly and said, "How about we never speak?" He replied, "Never, Darlene?" I said yes, never. I also told him if he ever needs to ask me anything concerning the job, don't hesitate, but we will never do the pleasantries. He just looked at me in shock and walked off.

Here are my thoughts on that situation: You're not going to dictate how crappy you treat me, whenever you feel like it. How about we never speak again? How about that?

What I noticed about some-timey people who want to ignore you as if they didn't see or hear you speak to them: They can dish it out, but they can't stand being ignored because as soon as I gave them a dose of their own medicine, they wanted to start speaking again. The difference between me and them is once you get me to that point, I can cut you off for years and forever, and not be mad at you either. I'm just not fooling

with you and they can't take it: they look all mad
with their face turned up.

I Spy

Sometimes drama would be going on that I wouldn't know about. This African American lady named Nicole was a secretary whom I had known for years on the job. Nicole had a very close Latino friend named Delilah, a mechanic whose husband was a mechanic at a different division. Nicole had a crush on a mechanic named Fred. Sometimes I would see Fred and Delilah sitting in the bus in the dark talking. It did look suspect, but I didn't think much of it, being that Delilah was married. I just thought they were trying to hide from their supervisors.

One day Nicole came up to me and asked if I ever saw Fred and Delilah talking a lot to each other. I told her yes. I figured by this time Nicole and Fred were dating and maybe she wanted to know what was going on with Fred and Delilah. I continued to see them sitting in the bus in the dark talking. I didn't have to go out of my way to see them. They seemed very comfortable with each other. I couldn't believe it because Delilah was married, and I thought Delilah and Nicole were such good friends.

A week later, Nicole asked me if they were still talking to each other. I said yes. I've known Nicole for a long time, so I told her the truth. Nicole had this stern look on her face and just said OK. I don't know what happened with the three of them and their friendship, but Nicole and Fred must have worked things out because they got married and they are still married to this day.

Slip'n on the Job

I worked graveyard shift as a service attendant for seven years. Bus drivers that finished their bus run around 11 p.m. would pull into the yard with the interior lights off. The drivers normally pulled the bus up to the fuel island, parked, checked the bus (supposedly), grabbed their belongings and jumped off the bus. It's a service attendant's job to drive the bus into the fuel lanes to service the bus. As I started servicing the bus, I entered the bus number into the computer and pushed the button on the blower to turn it on. The blower extended to the front door of the bus. I put the fueling nozzle into the fuel tank, checked the oil and water. Then I grabbed the hose, which is connected to a long air wand. When I squeezed the lever on the air wand, air pressure came out and now I was ready to blow all the trash inside the bus starting from the back to the front and into the blower that sucks up the trash.

Sometimes bus drivers didn't check their buses before they hopped off to go home. When I entered the back door of the bus to blow the trash into the blower, I didn't expect to see a drunk passed out on the bus. It was so dangerous because I never knew when something like that was going to happen. I was always startled. Sometimes the drunk or homeless person was startled by me. They didn't hear me telling them to get off the bus. Usually it was a harmless and surprised man (sometimes a woman) who couldn't figure out where they were. They'd been out with friends and had a few too many and missed their stop and ended up asleep dead drunk on the bus. Sometimes it was a homeless person, maybe meek and apologizing and trying to disappear into the night as quietly as possible, and sometimes not so quiet but confused and singing garbled Christmas carols and acting offended that I asked them to get off the bus.

I really didn't know if the bus driver was slip'n on the job or if they just didn't care because they were in a rush to go home. It was the driver's job to check their buses and to make sure there were no passengers left on the bus before entering the bus yard.

With all of the encounters I had with drunks and homeless passengers, I'm thankful to God that I never got hurt.

FAKE CAKE AND ICE CREAM

At my division, my co-workers came up with the idea to celebrate birthdays with cake and ice cream. The day of the party, someone from the clique would go around to every service attendant and ask for five dollars toward the cake and ice cream for the birthday person. I might have thought it was a great idea to celebrate people on their birthdays if I wasn't in a room with a bunch of fakes!

I used to go to all of the birthday parties and gave the amount of money the person asked for, until one day I had enough of giving my money and time to go around people that didn't like me and - as quiet as it was kept - they didn't even like each other. A co-worker asked me if I was going to the birthday party and I said, "No, I don't want any fake cake and ice cream." My co-worker looked at me with an expression on her face like "Did she just say that?" I didn't have to explain what "fake cake and ice cream" meant. She understood exactly what I was saying, and I didn't care what the clique thought about it either. I let it be known I was sick of the clique and I'm wasn't about to sit and eat cake and ice cream with people who pretended to be cool with me, and soon as the party was over, they are throwing darts in my back. No Thank Youuuuu! Co-workers that don't like you will ask you for money in a heartbeat to accomplish their goal for a successful party, but they will not get MY money and time. They can eat fake cake among themselves. (LOL)

When I was pregnant, I worked at Gateway. Metro has a program for pregnant women so they can work in an office. I was in the program because I didn't want to take the chance of breathing in diesel fuel from buses. Awesome program!

I worked in the Human Resources Department with this nice, timid lady. It was a huge office with cubicles, and everyone was nice to me and made me feel welcome. One of the higher-up lady bosses came to the office I worked in and told everyone: "I want a birthday party!" My mouth flew open. Did this lady just tell everyone to give her a party! (OMG) At the division on the yard, if someone in charge told us to give them a party, it wouldn't have happened. That's the difference between working at a division on the yard and working in office politics.

The day of the party, the nice lady I worked with did not want to go to the party. You know me. I said, "Well, don't go if you don't want to." She said, "I must go. If I don't, the boss might get mad at me."

I didn't understand that. I feel if you don't want to go to a party, you shouldn't have to. So, as everyone was leaving the office to attend this lady's fake party that she told everyone to give her, my boss invited me to go. Damn. I got to go eat some fake cake and ice cream. (LOL)

NEW BOOTIES

My co-workers were notorious for bad behavior; they plotted, they schemed, and they tried to recruit others to get on their conniving bandwagon. Months later those same people tried to befriend me as if nothing has ever happened. I didn't care how many months had gone by, I hadn't forgotten their crafty ways and bad behavior towards me, so there was no way I would befriend them. I never did anything to warrant their ill feelings toward me. In fact, I didn't know them at all. They were new hires and had only been working a month when my coworkers started campaigning against me.

Instead of calling them rookies I called them "new booties" because they were still on probation. They were nice the first few weeks until my messy co-workers got in their ears. It didn't bother me because I can't stand followers. If they thought for themselves, they would not have treated me like they did. It's so many weak-minded people that love being a part of a clique, and when they get to know you and see that you're not like what they've heard, they still go along with the nonsense so they don't become an outcast from the clique.

Years ago, I decided I would never let my co-workers verbally disrespect me. They can talk about me and hate me from afar, but they know better than to bring that mess to me. I advise anyone new coming into this field or any work environment where cliques exist to take time to know your job and what's expected of you and get to know the people you work with. Because going in blind may have you slipping on your job and/or grouping up with a clique of fake friends.

Snap Crackle Pop

One day, one of the supervisor's pets - Danna aka Pufferfish - was feeling herself. I named her Pufferfish because she would always come to work with her mouth and jaws poked out. On her first day on the job, I tried to be friendly and say hi to her but she had this stank expression on her face that read "Stay away from me!" But I noticed she had a very inviting attitude toward the men on the job.

Over time, she seemed to be friendlier towards me until one day another co-worker and I had a disagreement about something and Danna quickly jumped on the bandwagon. Through the years she would act as if she had a problem with me, she would talk about me behind my back. But when her friends weren't around, she would try to hold a conversation with me and I would engage. I even invited her to my wedding. Initially she wasn't invited but I could tell she wanted an invite bad because all of my other co-workers were invited. She would speak to me sometimes, and sometimes she wouldn't.

After years of this type of behavior I just got tired of it. One day we were in the locker room and she said "Hi, Darlene." I responded, "Look, either we're going to speak to each other or not because all this 'sometimes' speak is not going to work; it throws me off."

As time went on, she stopped speaking to me because the clique didn't speak to me. Then to my surprise, I was in the locker room getting ready to go home when she walked in with tears in her eyes. She just started talking to me about how bad her boyfriend was treating her. I encouraged her and gave her advice. It was time for me to go home, but I stayed and continued to talk to her until she stopped crying and felt better.

This is the same lady that told people not to speak to me and for years caused confusion on the job. Her bad behavior wasn't just toward me; it was also toward her job responsibilities, which she slacked on.

She was one of the supervisor's pets that didn't have to work, so instead of her getting a bus to clean and taking it to the steamer so he could clean the floor and back wall, she was riding around the yard not doing anything. Every day she basically came to work to log down already cleaned buses as if she cleaned them herself. I already knew the supervisor kept allowing her and some of his other pets to take credit for already clean buses. Eventually we were going to have a yard full of dirty buses. I made sure to keep a dated record of all the buses I cleaned.

Every day after Danna logged down a bus that was already cleaned, she would take a car-unit and drive to IHOP – International House of Pancakes. She did this daily and eventually she started gaining weight. I could see something deeper was going on with her and I knew the fake friends in her clique could tell too, yet no one said anything. She thought it was cute eating all of that food every morning. That's the only time she looked happy.

Our supervisor knew she was leaving the premises to buy breakfast, everyone knew. He also knew she was picking already clean buses to log down as if she cleaned the bus so she could sit down and then go out for food, but he would never admit it because then he would have to admit that he wasn't doing his job. We had a fleet of filthy buses because the supervisor created these little monsters and allowed their bad behavior to go on for so long that it called attention to his boss Cred.

So now that his butt was on the line, he decided to call a mandatory meeting with all service attendants. We all met up in the conference room. The meeting was about the fleet of dirty buses in the yard. I was already sitting at a table with the other service attendants when Danna aka Pufferfish and her friend Slim came in. They looked around and saw there were no more seats available, so Slim sat on the edge of the table where I was sitting. Then Pufferfish decided she was going to do what Slim did, but when she sat on the edge of another table, the whole table flipped up and everyone started laughing. She even laughed at herself.

Everyone had stopped laughing except for me, I was still laughing. I know, I know, I was doing too much but she got on my last nerve anyway. Danna looked at me with a stern look and said, "It's not that funny." When she said that to me, I think subconsciously I had been waiting in the cut to let her have it for being so mean and two-faced. She stabbed me in the back over and over through the years. I cut off my laugh immediately and gave her the death stare and said, "It was funny to me."

My supervisor went on with the meeting, saying everyone had to start early and have their buses cleaned by the end of their shift. Danna then spoke out and said, "Darlene always gets her bus steamed first." When I heard my name come out of her mouth, that's when I did a snap crackle pop on her ass. I interrupted her and said, "First of all, if you weren't riding around the yard in circles lollygagging maybe you could get your bus steamed early. You don't get your bus steamed first because you don't want to. Don't try to use me as your scapegoat."

Everyone in the conference room got quiet, including the supervisor; you could hear a pin drop. It was like I took over the meeting and it didn't stop there. I told her, "You don't come to work to work, you come to sit on your butt all day and eat the whole House of Pancakes."

Then I went in a different direction and told her: "You're a joke and I don't respect you. I started rambling, saying it doesn't make sense eating all of those pancakes and bacon every day. I said, "Something is wrong with you. You have a problem with eating and eating and eating." I stood up and said, "You're lazy and trifling."

At this point she didn't say anything, and everyone in the conference room was in shock, including her clique. I was loving it because I got to tell her off in front of her fake friends. When I was done giving her a piece of my mind, the supervisor ended the meeting.

As I began to walk out of the conference room, Danna stood up and came walking after me and asked, "What did you say to me?" Everyone got out of their chairs as if there was going to be a fight. I did an about-face, looked her in her eyeballs and repeated, "I said, 'you are lazy and trifling.'" She didn't say anything else. Maybe she was in shock. I don't know what made her think that I wouldn't say it again.

One of my co-workers who's a jokester said, "You guys stop, you're supposed to be Christians!" Then Danna said, "That's the problem! Everybody thinks she's a Christian." I said, "You didn't say that when you were in the locker room crying to me about your man." Danna's clique looked shocked because they didn't know she was talking to me. The look on their faces read, "Girl, you in the locker room crying to Darlene?" and the look on my face read "Yes, she did."

I know that Dana hated that I put her on blast in front of her so-called friends. She didn't want them to know that. I was told later that after I left the conference room, she started crying and the supervisor said to her, "The truth hurts." Now this is coming from the man who helped create the monster she had become.

Normally I'm reserved and don't like bringing attention to myself, but sometimes you have to step out the box and let a person know: I'm not the one to be played with. I know Danna wished that day could start over again after she got checked in front of her friends.

For the next couple of months when my co-workers saw me, they would joke and say, "Who are you hoo-riding on today?" I would just smile and keep it moving. I had other co-workers explaining to me why they're eating so little (and not at IHOP!) because they didn't want me to talk about them the way I did Danna! (LOL!)

They were just joking, but I heard one of her own friends asked her: "You're not being trifling, today, are you?" I believe she got annoyed for that day for a long time.

THE STANK IS REAL

Unfortunately, my co-workers and I knew which bus drivers had stinky booty. The bus driver would pull up right before the fueling station and leave the bus running with the parking brake on. Then he would hop off the bus and go home. Once the driver was gone, I would get on the bus, drive into the fuel lane and service the bus.

On some of the buses I would drive into the fuel lanes, the driver's seat would STINK. The buses from the 1980s had small, breathable holes in the seats with a cushion inside the leather seats so all the funk from the driver working eight to twelve hours a day went down to the cushion. When I got on the bus and sat in the driver's seat, all of that funk would come up to my nose, the worst smell ever!

The drivers I knew that had stinky booty, I would place the small bus trash bag on the seat and sit on top of it. And if the 1980s buses didn't have trash bags, I would sit on the edge of the driver's seat using only my left foot to operate the brakes and accelerator pedal. I learned how to pull the bus into the fuel lane that way because I didn't want to sit in that funk.

That's not the worst of it! Transit drivers would pee in the small bus bags and tie them loosely sometimes and leave it between the driver's window and the dash board, or they would leave the bag of pee in the back of the bus under the seat. Yes, the drivers would go to the back door stairs, step down and pee. Some of my co-workers when they blew the trash out the bus with the air-wand, the air pressure from the wand hitting against the loosely tied bag of pee would cause splatter. I never experienced pee splatter. I would take the long air-wand and lift the bag of pee and throw it into the blower. I knew where the drivers liked to hide the bag of pee and I would use low air pressure in those areas just in case there was a bag full of pee there.

Now the other monster was the vomit left on the bus from passengers. Soon as I walked on the bus, I could smell it! We call it a "sick bus." I couldn't stand to look at it so I would place a bunch of thick paper towels over it and sweep it into the tall dust pan, then I would get a mop and bucket filled with hot water, bleach and red soap and clean it up. When I was done cleaning, I would steam-clean the broom and dustpan.

I hated "sick buses" and I hated to see beer cans in the back of the bus. As I used the air-wand to blow the trash to the front of the bus, I would see beer cans rolling on the floor to the front along with everything else and I'd be thinking to myself: "Please please don't let beer spill out of those cans because old beer stink so bad!"

Sometimes blowing trash out the bus with the air-wand, I would see the disgusting things passengers leave on the back of the bus: dirty syringe needles, used condoms, and sometimes feces! I had enough seniority not to have to clean the feces! Phew!

When the company was RTD, it was some strange goings-on in the back of the bus. I'm sure the cameras on the buses help to minimize the crazy things that used to happen on the bus. But drivers! You still have to wash your butt and take restroom breaks when you can!

Finally Enough

My supervisor Bryson was so unfair to me. He took pride in doing favors for service attendants and mechanics so he could turn around and ask you to do something that wasn't in the job description. He would give his clique any day off they asked for even though he wasn't supposed to let more than two people off at a time. I made sure I didn't ask him for any special favors so he couldn't ask me to do something outside of my classification. I believe he didn't like that about me and I didn't sit in the office around him like some of the other employees.

I cleaned two interior buses a day five days a week while his favorites were allowed to take credit for buses that were already cleaned. It would upset me, but I had no time to worry about what they did or didn't do; I was there to do my job and go home. I started documenting the date and time of every bus I cleaned because I knew eventually my division was going to have a yard full of dirty buses again.

Supervisor Bryson - who didn't seem to care about passing cleanliness inspections - would inspect my buses every day at the end of my shift.

He made sure I was assigned the dirtiest buses, yet he never inspected buses that his clique supposedly cleaned. Any job that his clique didn't want to do, I had to do it and I had the highest seniority out of all the other service attendants. This went on for a year. He also had service attendants watch me and report to him the amount of times I went to the restroom and locker room, and he had them time me so he'd know how long I was in there. No matter how well I cleaned the buses he assigned me and no matter how much I stayed out of his way, he continued to mess with me.

Coming to work was very stressful. I never knew what to expect from him. I started getting headaches more frequently every day, the back of my skull was hurting, my eyes would twitch uncontrollably and the top of my shoulders were in so much pain, I could feel the knots. I couldn't go to my manager; it would have made things worse for me. So, I got an attorney and sued the company for harassment and stress.

I had no other choice; this supervisor wouldn't stop harassing me. I felt I had to fight back for my rights. I was angry. I had to sue the company and take time off to heal myself mentally and physically. I had to get physical therapy for my back and shoulders and I had to see another doctor for pain in the back of my skull.

I also talked with a therapist about what I had been going through with my supervisor on the job. She asked me if I thought Bryson had a crush on me and was trying to get my attention like a little boy in school that sits behind a little girl that he likes and keeps pulling on her ponytail. At that time, the last thing I wanted to hear in the same sentence was my supervisor liking me, so I told her, no, I don't think he likes me. In my mind I thought, "How could he like me or try to get attention from me when he's dogging me out every day? The last thing I'm going to do is give him attention."

The therapist suggested I transfer to a different division and I told her, no, I'm not going anywhere. I worked for this company and this division for years before he started working for the company. Why can't upper management just make him stop harassing me?

It's a shame I had to sue the company. I won my harassment case. I was off work for almost a year and, when I went back to work, my supervisor never harassed me again. As a matter of fact, when I did decide to transfer, it was on my terms, not because I let my supervisor run me out of my division. I transferred to another location and supervisor Bryson gave a good recommendation to my new supervisor Bob. Bob told me that Bryson said, "She's a good worker, just leave her alone and she will do her job!"

ALL FOOD AIN'T GOOD FOOD

Tina and I would walk across the street to this hamburger stand during lunch break. Sometimes I would treat her to lunch and sometimes she would treat me. Until one day I noticed my white coverall back pockets were rising higher on my butt. So I had to cut down on eating fast food and start watching my diet so I didn't bust out of my uniform. I was a size eight and Tina was a size fourteen.

Soon after, Tina asked me to walk with her to the hamburger stand. I said OK. When we got there, she walked up to the window. The man asked, "Can I take your order?" After she ordered the double chili cheeseburger and onion rings, Tina looked at me and said, "Order what you want - my treat!"

I had told Tina earlier that week that I was cutting down on fast food because I gained some weight. So I looked at Tina and said, "I don't want anything." She looked at me as if I asked her to order me everything on the menu. Then she gave me a side-eye look as to say: Oh, you don't want to eat because you're watching your weight. Too good to have the avocado double cheeseburger and the double cheese fries and a milk shake with the triple chocolate with your friend Tina because yo' ass is getting big." I was thinking to myself: "So what if I don't want to order a burger as big as my head just so you won't feel so bad about all the junk food you're eating. Why do you have an attitude?" Then a light bulb came on in my head. "Oh, that's exactly it, isn't it? You want me to gain weight! That's what the side-eye with attitude is about!"

Ladies, watch out for the Tinas of the world.

SOME-TIMEY CO-WORKERS

I never understood why Metro employees were so some-timey. The men and women both acted this way. When I was younger, this type of behavior threw me off. I never knew if the person was going to speak or not, even when I said hi or good morning first. I summed it up as "It's a game" and after 32 years with the company, I gamed out. I would not put up with the foolishness.

You have some people say hi one day who then won't acknowledge you the next day. Believe it or not, some people get a kick out of you speaking to them first so they can ignore you. They will walk right by you with their big head turned the opposite direction so they don't have to speak or acknowledge you. I also had co-workers that would turn up their noses and eyebrows to let you know "I don't like you or care for you."

  Soon as you take back your power and leave them alone and don't put yourself in a position to be ignored by them, that's when they want to start speaking and saying hi to you as a way to let you know it's okay for you to speak to them ... so they can ignore you again. Crazy, right?

Don't let people bait you back in to snub you, and don't have attitude about it either just give them a dose of their own medicine. Leave them alone and don't give them your energy. Don't be surprised if they try to speak to you. It's up to you to give them another chance. Personally, I no longer play that game. Once you show me you're a fool, I treat you accordingly. I ignore fools and only deal with them regarding the job. As soon as some-timey co-workers figure out I could care less about speaking to them, they always want to start speaking to me. Some-timey people can't stand to be ignored.

Rainy Night

I was working graveyard shift. The shift started at 11p.m. This particular night it was raining hard. Normally, if it's raining, the swing shift crew would sit inside a bus after they had finished servicing the buses. This rainy night the swing shift crew was standing in the fuel island and the sheriffs were everywhere. My shift had just started so I asked a co-worker what was going on.

He said Kace and Daniel were arrested for stealing money out of the bus fareboxes. I was in shock because Kace and I started together in the graffiti program for youths and we were the first group to become service attendants for RTD. I couldn't believe Kace would put himself in this position. He had recently gotten married and had twins.

One of the sheriffs told my supervisor that Kace was fast. He said when Kace saw them coming, he jumped out of the back window on the bus and ran down the bus lane trying to get away. RTD buses had large windows in the back that you could unlock and push out.

The sheriff said they had been watching them for months. The old fareboxes are different from the ones you see on the buses now. You could pry open the top of the old fareboxes with a tool. Kace and Daniel would put the buses with the fullest fareboxes on a certain lane on nights they figured service attendants and mechanics wouldn't be walking around in the yard, and because it was pouring down rain, they thought no one would be watching them. Little did they know the sheriffs were waiting. I was so disappointed and sad for Kace because he blew such a good opportunity with RTD and I know his family was counting on him.

Shop Steward

I've had only a handful of good shop stewards over the years - Lowell, Mosby, Jim, etc. I'm so thankful for my ATU. The union has fought for its members' rights and wages. Lowell was my first shop steward. He was so professional and fought for the members' rights. He was fair and did not pick and choose who he would fight for. I sure missed him when he retired.

As the years went on, we started getting different kind of shop stewards, you know, the kind that's not for the union members and is in the pockets of supervisors and managers. If the shops steward knew the supervisor or manager wanted to fire you or suspend you, the shop steward wouldn't fight as hard for you in a hearing. In return for selling you out, the shop steward could take off work at a whim. The shop steward didn't have to put in a request form to take the day or week off.

Oh yes, and you also have the types of shop stewards that are in messy cliques. Just know whatever personal issues you are having on or off the job that's affecting your job performance, we all know about it because the shop steward has told your business to the clique. Shop stewards are supposed to be in your corner and not giving away your strategy to the supervisor. You have some rotten-to-the-core shop stewards that will not support you so they can gain favor with the supervisors. The shop stewards that act this way don't throw everyone under the bus, just the employees they either don't like or the supervisor, manager or the clique doesn't like.

If you don't trust your shop steward, you can call the union office and put in a request for a union officer to represent you in a hearing with the manager. Sometimes that could be a problem because the union officer doesn't know you or why you're bypassing the shop steward. Your shop steward will give the union officer information that's not favorable about you. Most union officers don't get caught up in the division drama bit. It's up to you to tell the union officer your side first and why you'd like to be represented by a union officer instead of your shop steward. So when he does speak to your shop steward, whatever lies or half-truths they tell, he will be able to have a better understanding why you want him to represent you.

I had a shop steward named Linda; she might think she knows why I never came to her for advice when I had an issue on the job. I never went to her because I didn't trust her. My co-worker shared with me years ago that Linda told around her good friend's personal financial business and tax situation. In all fairness, how could I ever trust her with anything personal and trust she wouldn't blab it. If she'd reveal discreet talk about her own friend, she wouldn't think twice about me. Metro employees, don't play yourself. If you know your shop steward is messy, talks too much and is always taking lunch and cigarette breaks with the supervisor, call your union office for help.

Exposed

We all have them, on the job. On my job, you had a lot of them, from the Maintenance Department to Transportation and management. That's right, I said management.

When I was first hired at RTD, they told us what uniform we would be wearing and where to purchase steel-toed shoes. Service attendants didn't have to pay for the uniforms and steel-toed shoes. Bus drivers had to be in uniform and management has to set a good example and dress professional on the job. Service attendants could either wear a shirt and pants or coveralls; the supervisor asked you your size and he ordered the uniform.

Bus drivers had to go buy their uniforms. So why is it some women service attendants and bus drivers wore their pants so tight that they had a camel toe? Could it be to catch men's attention? And if that was the reason, why would you want to draw that type of attention on the job? It's unprofessional!!

A lady in management, Alice, worked out, I think, because her little ass weighed a buck-oh-five. Alice thought it was OK to wear short-

shorts walking on the premises in an environment that had a majority of men working.

When I first saw her dressed like this, I started laughing to myself, thinking: Alice is crazy and she does this all the time. I understand she wanted to get her walking in, but I had never seen this before from management. It just looked odd to me. I honestly think she was oblivious.

Now this other lady, I think she was literally crazy and thirsty for attention. She had on her uniform; her buttons were unfastened to the middle of her chest. She was a busty woman. I caught myself looking out for her and letting her know her buttons were open and you could see her breasts. She looked at me and said, "If they haven't seen titties by now.." and kept her shirt unbuttoned. That's when I knew she was crazy as hell. (Ha!) She came to work a lot with her shirt unbuttoned down to the middle of her chest with her boobs out. There is a time and place for everything, and on the job is neither the place nor the time to be exposed.

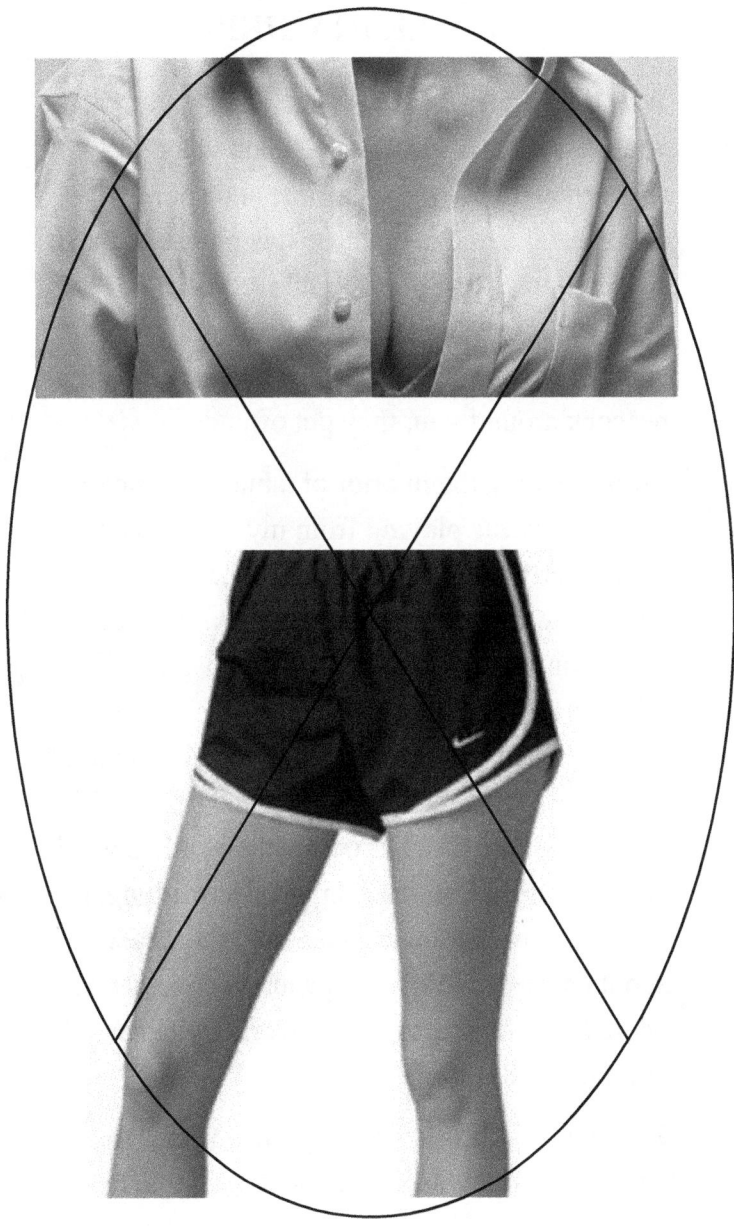

SISTER IN CHRIST

Why do people like to use this phrase: "I thought you were a sister in Christ?" when you don't allow them to invade your time and space? It's almost as if some people use this phrase to make you feel pressured into something you don't want or feel comfortable doing. So, when you don't allow some men to hug you or behave like a fool peacock around you, they get offended.

I was cleaning the interior of a bus and listening to gospel music playing from my boombox when the property maintenance man came to my division to fix the broken wash rack. He decided to step on my bus and introduce himself and asked if I were Christian. (I guess he asked me that because I had my gospel music playing loud on my bus.) I said, "Yes, I am" and he said, "I am a Christian, too." From that day, whenever he had to come to my division to fix something, he would always get on my bus, say hi and talk about church. We'd have general conversation while I was working. My co-worker nicknamed him Plumber Boy.

Then one day he came on my bus to say hi and during the conversation he mentioned that he owns a home in the San Fernando Valley. I said that was nice, but I was wondering why he told me that. Is it because he is trying to impress me? After he left my bus, I didn't think about it anymore because I wasn't attracted to him at all and I know I didn't have to see him every day.

About six months later I transferred from my division to another location. This location was huge and a lot of people with different classifications and positions worked there. Plumber Boy worked there. It was his home location, so that meant I would be seeing him a lot more. (Oh, boy!)

When Plumber Boy saw me and learned that I transferred over, he was so excited! Every time he saw me, he would literally wave his hands in the air like a landing-signal officer and grin like he was at the dentist. I don't like a lot of attention drawn to me in front of people so when he would act like this, I was embarrassed.

One of my co-workers would tease me while he was trying to flag me down with his hands and she would say jokingly, "There is your boyfriend!" because she knew it got on my nerves when he would act so animated. During my break I was sitting with my co-worker Mark out on the patio. I got up to go buy a muffin from the cafeteria and ran into Plumber Boy, and there he goes acting all extra animated again. I said hi and asked him not to be so extra extra when he sees me and to just say hi or good morning.

I left the cafeteria and sat with my co-worker on the patio and began to eat my muffin. I looked around and Plumber Boy was standing next to me, eyes blood-shot red. He looked at Mark and said, "Excuse me, brother, no disrespect to you," then he looked at me and said "I thought you were a sister in Christ."

I can't even tell you what all Plumber Boy said to me. I just kept a smile on my face and asked him, "Are you done yet?" and told him he could leave now. I didn't want to make a big scene on the patio full of my co-workers, but I couldn't wait until my break was over. I wanted to take my left hand and choke his neck so I waited until the break was over.

I found Plumber Boy and told him, "Don't you ever approach me and disrespect me like that again! From this day forward, don't speak to me, don't even look at me!" and I walked off. One good thing came from him tearing his drawls with me. I no longer had to look at him portraying a landing-signal officer.

TOWN CRIER

Ladies and gentlemen, we have town criers that work for Metro. These are the people you don't want tell to anything to if you don't want the information to get out. I think it's pitiful when a man does this. Real men don't have time to gossip or carry news about someone else's business. Some Metro men are some of the most bitch-made men that I don't care to know. They are worse than women. I know this because I have always worked around mostly men. They carry news and lies.

I've witnessed the town crier tell everyone:

What you guys did after work;

How you made a fool out of yourself at the gentleman's club;

How you're married but got turned down by other women;

How many DUI's you have;

How dirty the inside of your home is;

How your wife has a sink full of dirty dishes;

How broke you are;

How your kids and grandkids are f**k-ups;

How you have other women on the side;

How you lost your home;

That you live in a bad area;

How they don't like hanging out with you after work;

That you have hepatitis and you shouldn't be helping make food at work;

How you punch in late;

How you left work early;

That you're an alcoholic and on Step 5;

How your wife left you for another man;

That you failed a drug test;

How you were sleeping during work hours;

How you come to work with alcohol on your breath;

That the IRS is garnishing your check;

I've seen and heard the town crier spread personal information about people right after they've vowed to keep information to themselves. Be mindful who you share your personal information with because the town crier has no loyalty to anyone.

Fifty Hands

Some Metro employees are touchy feely. I was wearing a bulky, blue Metro jacket made from the same material as my blue overalls. Metro gave me the jacket years ago. When I transferred to my new work location, a mechanic asked me where I got the jacket. I said the company gave it to me. As we were walking through the parking lot to go home, he asked me what size was my jacket and before I could get it out, this fool flipped my collar inside out to see the size of my jacket. It took everything in me not to sock him with my fist. I continued to walk to my car and go home. I was so furious he put his hands on me without my permission.

The next day after I had calmed down, I walked up to him and asked if he remembered flipping my collar inside out. He said yes. I told him: "Don't ever do that again, I don't like people touching me without my permission." His face went from a smile to shock to pissed off. I'm the one who should be pissed, you invaded my personal space!

When I have called out some men for hugging or touching me, they either apologize or they get an attitude with me for calling them out.

A man that worked in the storeroom was walking toward me but just before we passed, he swung his right hand in front of my vagina as if he was going to touch me down there. I stopped and asked him, "What are you doing? Don't you ever put your hand in front of me again." Of course, he got mad and walked off.

There was another incident, this time with another service attendant. It was the beginning of my shift and I was having coffee and conversation with one of the mechanics. All of the mechanics were either drinking coffee or just talking to each other. This service attendant, Timothy, decided he's going to show off in front of the other men and put his arm around my shoulder and said good morning. I shrugged his arm off me and shouted, "Don't touch me!" He jumped back fast as lightning. I wanted all the men standing near to hear me. Timothy looked so scared. I wanted all the men around me to know this would happen to them too if they put their hands on me.

Some of my good male friends I had known on the job for years I wouldn't greet with a hug because I didn't want other men to think it was OK to hug me if they wanted to. Until one day I thought to myself," I will allow my friends to greet me with a hug and the other men that I have no rapport with better not try it or they will get checked on the spot. I don't care who you see me hug."

A custodian put his arm around me, showing off in front of this man I was talking to. I calmly looked at him and asked, "When did you start putting your arm around me? I've been working with you for a long time and you've never approached me like this." He stepped back and said, "Oh I'm sorry." I looked away and continued my conversation with my co-worker.

Some women on the job don't mind if guys hug or put their arm around them, and that's OK if they don't have a problem with it. But I do, especially the guys that walk past you and give you a quick massage with one hand on your shoulder. Eww, I hate that! I worked with over fifty men. Can you imagine letting them hug you, massage your shoulders or put their hands on your back every day, five days a week, for thirty-two years? That's too much damn touching for me. So, men, please know your audience and don't assume every woman wants to be hugged, touched or massaged by you.

My Wife Is Black

By this time, I have some experience under my belt. I've been dealing with the company for eighteen years. I know how to handle myself in just about every situation dealing with Metro folks. Same game, different faces.

If you knew me at the time, you wouldn't think I had as much time as I did. Most employees as soon as they passed probation, they had this aura about themselves, you would think they had my eighteen years of experience and I had their five-year experience.

I was at a new Metro location and my co-workers and supervisors assumed I only had five years with the company. The supervisors would give me assignments they couldn't give to the other service attendants because they would give the supervisor a hard time. The supervisor would see me and think, "She doesn't look like she would make a fuss. I will ask her to do assignments that are not in her classification."

I did the assignments for a while until I learned who was who and how my new location operated. Six months later, my supervisor was replaced by another supervisor, Roman. He was short in stature. He definitely had the short man syndrome.

Roman was a mess. He would walk up to you without saying anything while you were working and just stand there and watch you. Or he would stand at a distance if he saw you talking to a co-worker for a few minutes. Roman wanted you to know he was watching until you and whoever you were talking to would stop talking. He would always have this intimidating look on his face as if you were supposed to run when you saw him. Oh, he loved to keep me busy working and at the same time he loved being in my face talking to me, sometimes for twenty to thirty minutes at a time. But if he saw me talking to someone else, his face would turn up as if I was doing something wrong.

He would act this way every day. The way he was trying to intimidate me with his frowned-up face, I knew I had to watch this guy.

Roman thought that because he was my supervisor, he could talk to me about unrelated work topics as long as he wanted to, but if a co-worker asked me how I was doing, it was a problem. I recognized this same kind of bully spirit from my former work location.

Roman would tell me I smelled good and he liked the perfume I was wearing. One day he decided to say to me: "My wife is black." He asked if I would like to see a picture of her in his office. I said OK. It was a glamour shot, the kind you take inside of a shopping mall.

Every day, this man was getting on my nerves and I had to bite my tongue because I didn't want the harassment from him to get worse. Every day at the beginning of the shift, this man would come and talk to me for twenty minutes about nothing. Four months later, I was able to bid into another building at the same location. Hooray! I was getting away from this little pest!

I had some peace for a while. Then the manager transferred supervisor Roman to my new building. (Damn, here we go.) I was not in the mood to put up with this man's foolishness. He started up again, walking up to me, talking for up to sometimes thirty minutes a day. If I was working, he would stop me from working to talk about nothing. I started feeling really uncomfortable, but I knew if I showed any expression that I did not want to talk to him, it was going to be a problem and make things difficult for me on the job.

But Roman made things difficult for me anyway. He wanted to hold me up from working so he could talk to me every day at the beginning of my shift and dog me out at the same time. By this time, I had nineteen or twenty years with the company. No one works eight hours at Metro but this man wanted me working every minute, except for my breaks. In all the years I had been working for this company, I've never had a supervisor give me a floor plan of the building I'm working and write on the floor plan how many minutes to work on each task and to follow this every day.

I went to my shop steward, showed him the floor plan and told him how this man has been harassing me and I would like to have a meeting with him, the manager and supervisor Roman. At the meeting the next day, I talked by myself in that meeting for about twenty minutes. I told the manager everything, with Roman and my shop steward right there, listening. I showed the manager the floor plan of the building I work in and told him how Roman had been harassing, intimidating, and bullying me for months, and how he told me I smell good and that his wife is black. I think my manager was in shock, and Roman had disbelief across his face. The shop steward just sat there and didn't open his mouth because he could see "Oh, she's got this." I told the truth. Not once did Roman interrupt me and say I was lying. He kept his trap shut for once.

Roman left me alone and things got better from that point. People who think they are smarter because of a title or their position always eventually get caught up in their own mess when they are not doing what's right. Roman underestimated me because he was a supervisor and I was a service attendant. What he didn't realize was that I'm a fighter. And I will always fight for my rights and he was not the first bully supervisor I had dealt with. Roman, I can see your type from a mile away. Different face, same game.

A Fool

I once heard a man say, "A fool will teach you how to treat him." I didn't find out what that really meant until I met this man on the job named Cooper.

He worked on the buses. I should have gone with my first instinct after he asked me how many kids I had, and when I told him I had one child, he replied, "Are you sure?" as if he knew something about me I didn't know and that I was lying to him. It pissed me off a little, and normally when someone I don't know says something crazy to me, I just cut them off. But I let it go. He told me that someone told him that I had nine kids. I told him, "If I had nine kids, I would tell you." He felt embarrassed because he really believed what his co-worker told him. (Metro folks will lie and make up stories about you.) Now he knows I'm looking at him like a fool.

After that we became really good friends. I bought "The Bible Experience" for him and his wife. I thought it was a cool gift for his family, and Cooper and his wife bought me a scarf for Christmas.

A year later I asked Cooper if he could help my brothers move my furniture into my new place. He said yes, and once they finished moving all my furniture in, I asked Cooper to take me to get something to eat for everyone. We brought the food back and once my brothers were done eating, they left. Cooper and I were still eating and talking. This was the first time we were alone off the job.

Cooper was getting ready to go and I walked him to the door and thanked him for taking the time out of his schedule. That's when he made a move on me. He hugged me tight and whispered in my ear. "Girl, you know I'm crazy about you." I pulled away and said, "I don't look at you like that. You are married and I only see you as a friend."

When he left, I was in shock because at work he never flirted or came on to me, but as soon as he had an opportunity to be alone with me off the job, he tried it. I began to get angry and was thinking: "I don't want to be friends with him anymore."

When I saw Cooper at work the following Monday, he apologized and said, "Sis, I'm sorry. I hope you can forgive me." It was awkward for a few days but I forgave him and we went back to having lunch breaks together talking, laughing, and cracking jokes. He was so cool and down to earth and he always treated me like a sister, but whenever he saw my supervisor, he would act different.

You could see it in his face. Cooper did not like my supervisor due to personal reasons. He would always tell me hateful things about my supervisor. I've never had a problem with my supervisor, and over the years my supervisor and I had built a good rapport. This did not sit well with Cooper. He began acting out of character with me and tried to convince me that no one respects my supervisor, and if people see me talking to him, they won't respect me either. I told him I don't care what people think about me; he's my supervisor, I have to talk with him. When I said that, Cooper's eyes turned red like the devil.

The more Cooper kept trying to tell me what to do concerning my supervisor, the more I had a problem with Cooper. I told him, "Don't let your hate for my supervisor ruin our friendship. I talk to whomever I want."

For a few months I was working under another supervisor, so my former supervisor would stop by and we would talk from time to time. This particular day, I needed to talk with my former supervisor, and he told me he would come back later to speak with me. It just so happened that when he came back to talk to me, I was already talking to Cooper. I told Cooper I would be right back and he looked at me, tightened his lips and said, "You better not go, you better not." I just couldn't believe my eyes and ears. I told him I would be back and got up to go speak with my former supervisor for a few seconds, and when the supervisor left, Cooper said to me: "Man, you're weak, you're weak!" and walked off. I stood there thinking, "What just happened?"

It was time to go home, and I was in the locker room getting my things together, getting angrier and angrier. Who the hell does he think he is speaking to me in that manner? I was done with that friendship.

For the next two weeks my shop steward was trying to mend my friendship with Cooper, but I wasn't budging. Then Cooper anonymously wrote letters to safety and other supervisors, slandering my name and character. He also left me a hateful voicemail. Cooper left me with no other choice but to defend myself.

I talked to my manager and a manager from a different department. I played the message Cooper left on my voicemail verbally attacking me and threatening me. I also showed both text messages left by Cooper on my cellphone and a printout sheet. They were shocked when they heard what he said on the voicemail and of his tone. He also had someone call and threaten my supervisor pretending to be my man. All the years I've worked for this company I have never had a family member or friend call my job on my behalf. My supervisor asked the man for his name. The man replied, "Looney Toon!" I'm thinking, "Oh my god, why me?" We couldn't prove it, but we knew Cooper was behind the phone call.

Then he left me another voicemail. After hearing his foolish, confusing and threatening message I thought, "Wow, what a crazy control freak!" His message was filled with lies and made no sense at all. I didn't know what he was talking about. After listening to the voicemails, it confirmed that he was crazy and delusional.

After he did all of this, he actually tried to talk to me. I told him, "I no longer want to be your friend. Don't call or text me again." Then I saw that crazy look in his eyes again, so I just walked away. I reported what happened to my manager and supervisor. I asked my manager to talk to him and to tell him to stay away from me, which my manager did, but Cooper made another attempt to talk to me. He was talking crazy to the point that I felt scared and uncomfortable, so I contacted the Metro police.

I thought, "If he isn't listening to me or our manager, maybe he'll listen to the police and stay away from me." I told the police everything that was going on, including the phone call to my supervisor. The police talked to Cooper and told him to stay away from me and if anything happened to me or my supervisor, they would be looking for him.

With all of the harassment, verbal attacks, spreading lies about me and leaving crazy voicemails, my manager only gave him a one-day suspension for his behavior, so it's no wonder he kept bothering me. There was no fear of consequences. If it had been another type of manager, Cooper would have gotten at least a thirty-day suspension with no pay or he would've been terminated.

After his one-day suspension, guess what? He harassed me again. He would come over to my work area and just stare at me with an intimating look and he called me trash. Sure, I could've cursed him out but I refused to give this man my energy.

I wrote him up again and this time I went over the manager's head and talked to another manager. Cooper went on a campaign slandering my name to everyone, telling more lies. Some of my co-workers that were normally friendly had stopped speaking to me.

Finally, the old manager was replaced. The new manager's nickname was Snake-Eyes. He was my manager in the past and he was a no-nonsense type of manager. If he had been the manager when Cooper was acting a fool, he would have been fired or he would've received a 30-day suspension. People like Cooper play crazy, but he heard about Snake Eyes, and Cooper dealt with it by telling my supervisor he didn't want to talk to him unless a shop steward was around, and Snake Eyes sent another manager around to tell

Cooper my supervisor could talk to him anytime he wanted without a shop steward.

After that, Cooper had been very quiet and kept to himself because he knew he couldn't play the games he had played with the other manager. If Snake Eyes was there when Cooper was acting a fool with me, I guarantee it wouldn't have gone as far as it did. Basically, Cooper left me alone because he knew Snake Eyes would not tolerate his foolishness.

PRINCESS OF METRO

Some of my co-workers sarcastically put me on this pedestal and called me "the princess." Most of the service attendants I worked with were older than me but I had more seniority than them. If there was a job assignment that no one wanted to do, the supervisor would ask for volunteers. If there weren't any, the person with the lowest seniority had to do the job. At that time, I had over twenty years with the company. I almost never had to do a job assignment that I didn't want to do because there was always someone with lower seniority. I was only required to do a job assignment I didn't bid for when someone of low seniority was on vacation and they were under-staffed.

My co-worker Giselle asked me if I would go into rotation with my other co-workers so she wouldn't have to clean interior buses so often. I said no because I had earned my seniority, and if I started going into rotation cleaning buses, the other service attendants were going to want me in rotation with other job assignments. Of course, she had an attitude about it, but I heard this same lady numerous times saying she didn't care who did the job assignment, but that was because she had more seniority than anybody else. So how can she be mad at me for not giving up my seniority on a daily basis?

Giselle was on a mission to get me to clean a bus; she would tell some of the supervisors that I never clean buses, saying, "Oh, the princess is too good to clean buses," which made the supervisors call me princess. Of course, not to my face but behind my back.

I bid on a job assignment I didn't mind doing every day, just like everyone else. I didn't want to go into rotation cleaning buses; that was a problem for her and a few other co-workers. I continued to do the job assignment I bid on for years. Through the years, different managers and supervisors came and went so they didn't know me or my work ethic; all they knew was my current supervisor was not complaining about me and I had never been written up on my work performance. You would think that would be enough. Nope. The Giselles of the world will make sure they taint your name to whomever will listen, and unfortunately some supervisors and managers believe everything they hear negative about an employee.

If we were short-handed and someone needed my help cleaning a bus, I had no problem with helping. My problem was the supervisor or manager jumping on board with Giselle. All of them were on a mission to see me cleaning buses every chance they got. They loved when we were short of employees so they could see Darlene clean a bus.

This happened a few times when I had to clean an interior bus. The service attendants would stand at a distance in a huddle watching me clean my bus. (Ridiculous.)

They called me the princess so much that I went to Party City and bought the prettiest tiara they had and wore it to work all day. I walked all around the premises to make sure the service attendants, supervisors and managers all saw it on top of my head. The co-workers that didn't know what was going on asked me if I was wearing the tiara because it was my birthday. I said, "No I'm wearing it because I'm a princess." You should've seen the looks and crooked smiles on Giselle and her clique. That was my way of letting them know that I knew what they had been doing and saying behind my back. I wasn't done with them yet.

If a service attendant bids for the steamer position, they cannot take you off that job to clean buses, no matter what. So, guess what. I did something they never thought I would do; I bumped a service attendant that was in the clique off his steamer position and there was nothing they could do about it. In this position, they couldn't pull me off steaming to clean buses whether they were short-handed or not. I also made more money as a steamer, so it was win-win for me.

After I bumped my co-worker off his steamer position, it caused a domino effect. Everyone was trying to figure out what position they would bid for. The look on Giselle and the clique's face was priceless. They got bumped off their cushy jobs.

The service attendants were saying I wouldn't be able to handle steaming bus engines and parts and that I would be calling in sick after six months because the job is so hard. What Giselle and her clique failed to realize was that when I started this job, I was nineteen years old with low seniority and I had to get under buses while they were on four lifts in the air, every night steaming off all the crud and oil from underneath the buses. I wore a head shield because crud would fall on my head. I did that every night because higher seniority didn't want to do it. I didn't have the luxury the steamers have now; with a push of a button the underground built-in washers will spray wash underneath the bus while you sit on the bus and wait for the machine to finish. So when I bumped my co-worker off the steamer position to steam engines and bus parts, it wasn't a problem for me.

I did my job well and I didn't take off work. I was the steamer for six months and showed everyone who doubted me that the steamer job is not as hard as some of the men had everyone believing and I can do any job because I have performed every service attendant job since I was nineteen years old. So yes, I am the Princess of Metro! Boom!

Diamonds Who Care

My immediate supervisor was out for the day so another supervisor filled in for him. His name was Austin. Before that day, I would sometimes see him in passing, but I had never been introduced to him. I called Austin and reported a situation I was still having with Cooper, and Austin said he would talk to him.

Later that day Austin thought this was a perfect opportunity to talk to me. This man held me up for thirty minutes in the sun talking about himself. He was a short stocky man with thin hair and a big ego. He wanted to let me know he's the man and my supervisor and he can get anyone to do a job because it's how you ask. So this fool gave me an example of what he meant.

Austin pointed to a pile of big rocks that had been placed in the yard by construction workers, and said, "If I asked you nicely to move those rocks, you would do it because I asked you nicely." I just looked at him and pretended I cared about what he was saying, but I didn't answer the question. What he was really trying to say was he could ask me to do anything and I would have to do it because he was my supervisor for the day. Austin was low-key flexing his authority.

Then he felt the need to inform me that he didn't have to knock on the door of the higher-ups on the 25th floor; he could just walk in because he's a Mason, just like one of the higher-ups. He also said a Metro employee wrote him up but nothing happened to him because of his affiliation.

Austin put his hand out to me to show me his rings and asked me, "Do you see this?" I said "yes," but his rings didn't look like much to me. Austin said, "These are diamonds and the other ring is a Mason ring and the higher-up on the 25th floor has one too."

I'm thinking to myself: "Fool, I don't care. It's hot out here while you're bragging about yourself and the masons. Well, whoopee! I could tell this man could be a potential problem. I recognize his type, a potential pest.

Later that week he saw me from a distance. I was on a fork lift and he was driving a cart. I was thinking, "Oh, S**t! This fool is going to try and hold me up again." His type will force their presence on you. Telling a person like him that you're busy and you have to get back to work, this can cause a problem for women.

I had picked up a metal can with the forklift. As I was about to back up, Austin swooped up behind me, blocking me from moving. I turned my head around and said hi, and he said hi, but for a few seconds he didn't say anything, he just started looking around.

Clearly, he didn't have anything to say to me. He looked at me as if I was supposed to start the conversation. I didn't say a word. He just wanted to be in my face. After a few seconds of awkward silence, he finally started talking, but it wasn't work related. I couldn't tell you what he was talking about. It went in one ear and out the other. I was too busy thinking, "Someone help me, this man has trapped me in and I can't go anywhere until he moves his cart." I had to stay and listen to his delusion of grandeur. This supervisor was so uncouth, I avoided him as much as possible unless it was work related.

The Red Wing truck would come to my work location; Metro employees could buy steel toe shoes off the truck. As I was buying a pair of steel-toe boots, Austin came over, lurking around. There were two ladies looking at shoes. One of the ladies was about to try on shoes when Austin asked her a stupid question in front of everyone:

"Wait, did you polish your toenails?" The lady replied, "Yes, I did." He replied, "Good girl!"

As a supervisor he shouldn't have asked her that question or referred to her as a "Good girl". He's so comfortable that he didn't think twice about asking her that in front of other employees. He needs to take a supervisor etiquette class.

No One But God

In spite of every negative thing I saw, heard and experienced at RTD/Metro, it wasn't all bad. There was a lot of good I experienced.

People are so amazed when I tell them I have worked for Metro 32 years. People can't believe I stayed with one company for that long.

I was able to work for RTD/METRO that long because God gave me this job, he put in me a conqueror spirit. When I look back over my career and all the good and bad things I went through, I think most people would have quit their jobs long ago. I always had the mind I would not let negative co-workers or management make me quit my job. I know and knew then at 19 years old that I'm blessed and it's up to me to push through trials, tests, phony friends, supervisors on a mission to write me up, slander, lies, and weariness. Some days I had to tell myself: You can do this Darlene. De'Onzae needs you, he's counting on you not to give up.

I would think about all the good things this job had afforded me to do, the ability to take care of my son and I, help family members, be a blessing to strangers, enjoy trips and adventures and the overall bigger picture. I have lifetime medical, a retirement plan, a pension and an IRA. These are the things I would think about and I was able to do it for 32 years. What I know now that I didn't know back then was, I always had the victory and I was going to come out victorious because God gave me the job and he would not put more on me than I could handle. Thank God for the Victory!

As I look back and reflect, I know it was no one but God.

No one but God gave me this peculiar career.

No one but God put it on Lena's mind to tell my mom about the Kenneth Hahn graffiti youth program.

No one but God knew my mom would tell me to apply for the graffiti program, which lead me opportunity to take the test for service attendant a year later.

No one but God knew positive people on my job would guide and help me through some rough patches.

No one but God gave me the perseverance to keep going when I wanted to quit working for Metro.

No one but God got me through the tears on the job.

No one but God gave me the strength to stand up for myself against my enemies.

No one but God blessed me with friendships on the job that I will always have long after I retire.

No one but God knew I would be able to retire from RTD/Metro at the age of 51 years old.

All glory be to God.

REFLECTIONS

pg. 106

www.ingramcontent.com/pod-product-compliance
Lightning Source LLC
LaVergne TN
LVHW041633070426
835507LV00008B/589